Contents

A friend is someone you can trust.

Making Friends

Cassie Mayer

www.heinemann.co.uk/library
Visit our website to find out more information about Heinemann Library books.

To order:
Phone 44 (0) 1865 888066
Send a fax to 44 (0) 1865 314091
Visit the Heinemann Bookshop at www.heinemann.co.uk/library to browse our catalogue and order online.

First published in Great Britain by Heinemann Library, Halley Court, Jordan Hill, Oxford OX2 8EJ, part of Harcourt Education. Heinemann is a registered trademark of Harcourt Education Ltd.

First published in paperback in 2008

Editorial: Cassie Mayer and Charlotte Guillain
Design: Joanna Hinton-Malivoire
Illustrated by Mark Beech
Art editor: Ruth Blair
Production: Duncan Gilbert

Printed and bound in China by South China Printing Co. Ltd.

ISBN 978 0 431 18680 1 (hardback)
11 10 09 08 07
10 9 8 7 6 5 4 3 2 1

ISBN 978 0 431 18688 7 (paperback)
12 11 10 09 08
10 9 8 7 6 5 4 3 2 1

British Library Cataloguing in Publication Data
Mayer, Cassie
Making friends. - (Citizenship)
1. Friendship - Juvenile literature
I. Title
177.6'2
A full catalogue record for this book is available from the British Library

Friends have fun together.

You can make friends by ...

asking someone to play with you.

You can make friends by …

telling someone you like them.

Good friends help each other.

Good friends care for each other.

A good friend …

takes turns choosing a game.

A good friend ...

shares her things.

A good friend …

listens to his friends.

A good friend …

says sorry when she is wrong.

It is important to be a good friend.

How can you be a good friend?

Activity

How is this boy being a good friend?

Picture glossary

share to let someone else use what you have; to give someone else a part of what you have

take turns give each person a chance to play something

Index

Note to Parents and Teachers

Before reading
Talk to the children about making friends and keeping friends. Ask them what things they like to do with their friends.

After reading
• Play the "We are friends" circle game. Ask the children to stand in a circle. Ask partners to face each other. They should hold out their right hands ready to shake hands. When they have shaken hands each child moves on round the circle in the direction they are facing to meet their next partner. They will shake left hands with this partner before moving on round the circle. As they move round they should say the rhyme: "Lucy's friends with Charlotte. Charlotte's friends with Joe. Joe is friends with everyone. And round our friends we go." Continue using the names of children in the class.
• Make a friendship circle. Using thick washable paint get the children to make hand prints. Then cut out the hand prints and place each in a large circle with little fingers overlapping. Write each child's name on their hand prints.